# SPEARFISHING MANUAL

Insider Secrets of Spearfishing
for Beginners to Die-Hard Spearos

By Mike McGuire

Copyright© 2014 by Mike McGuire - All rights reserved.

**Copyright**: No part of this publication may be reproduced without written permission from the author, except by a reviewer who may quote brief passages or reproduce illustrations in a review with appropriate credits; nor may any part of this book be reproduced, stored in a retrieval system, or transmitted in any form or by any means – electronic, mechanical, photocopying, recording, or other – without prior written permission of the copyright holder.

**Disclaimer**: The information within the book "Spearfishing Manual" is intended as reference materials only and not as substitute for professional advice. Information contained herein is intended to give you the tools to make informed decisions about your spearfishing skills and ability to freedive. Every reasonable effort has been made to ensure that the material in this book is true, correct, complete and appropriate at the time of writing.

The Author and Publisher has strived to be as accurate and complete as possible in the creation of this book, notwithstanding the fact that he does not warrant or represent at any time that the contents within are accurate due to the rapidly changing nature of the subject and the Internet (third party website links). Nevertheless the Author and Publisher assume no liability or responsibility for any omission or error, for damage or injury to you or other persons arising from the use of this material. Reliance upon information contained in this material is solely at the reader's own risk.

Any perceived slights of specific persons, peoples, or organizations are unintentional. This book is not intended as a substitute for the medical advice of physicians. Like any other sport, spearfishing poses some inherent risk. The Author and Publisher advice readers to take full responsibility for their safety and know their limits. It is also recommended that you consult with a qualified healthcare professional before beginning any training on the subject. Before practicing the skills described in this book, be sure that your equipment is well maintained, and do not take risks beyond your level of experience, aptitude, training and comfort level.

First Printing, 2014 - Printed in the United States of America

*"Shall I go to heaven or a-spearfishing?"*

# DEDICATION

To my father who taught me about amazing breathless adventure of spearfishing and peace of mind that is only found underwater.

# TABLE OF CONTENTS

| | |
|---|---|
| Introduction | 1 |
| Chapter 1 – What is Spearfishing? | 3 |
|     The Ancient Beginnings | 3 |
|     Newer Equipment | 5 |
|     Spearfishing Today | 6 |
| Chapter 2 – Methods of Spearfishing | 7 |
|     No Diving | 7 |
|     Shore Diving | 9 |
|     Boat Diving | 10 |
|     Blue Water Diving | 11 |
|     Freshwater Spearfishing | 12 |
|     Hole Diving | 13 |
|     Scuba Diving | 14 |
| Chapter 3 – Physical Fitness and Personal Preparation | 15 |
|     Your Body | 15 |
|     Training for Success | 17 |
|     Choose What Works for You | 19 |
|     Strength Training | 20 |

| | |
|---|---|
| Endurance Training | 26 |
| Flexibility Training | 27 |
| Controlled Breathing Exercises | 31 |
| Developing Presence of Mind | 33 |
| The Importance of Proper Preparation | 34 |
| Chapter 4 – How to Choose Guns, Tips and Spears | 35 |
| What is a Spear Gun? | 35 |
| Selecting the Right Gun for Your Needs | 44 |
| Categories of Spearfishing Spears and Guns | 46 |
| The Choices of Spear Tips | 50 |
| Chapter 5 – Other Equipment for Better Spearfishing | 53 |
| The Basics | 53 |
| And Beyond… | 58 |
| And Then Some… | 63 |
| Chapter 6 – Techniques and Tips for Spearfishing | 65 |
| What You Need to Know Before Hitting the Water | 65 |
| Spearfishing is a Science and an Art | 67 |
| Common Approaches to Catching Fish | 68 |
| Situations to Avoid | 71 |
| A Word About Safety | 72 |
| Samba and Shallow Water Blackouts | 74 |
| Chapter 7 – Hot Spots for Great Spearfishing | 77 |

| | |
|---|---|
| A Matter of Personal Preference | 77 |
| Frequently Recommended Locations | 78 |
| Conclusion | 85 |
| About the Author | 87 |

# INTRODUCTION

**Crystal clear water. A trophy fish. You, a spear gun and steady nerves.** With the advice in this book, some practice and a bit of luck, **this can be yours.**

Imagine a man in ancient times whose survival depended on his ability to hunt and catch food for the clan. He faced the unknown that was described by myths and legends of horrible creatures lurking in the depths. That same thrill can be achieved today in much the same way by practicing the sport of spearfishing. At the very least, spearfishing pits you, your skills and strength against the speed and agility of fish in their natural habitat. At the extreme, it tests your endurance, courage and willingness to push the limits in pursuit of a prize. It is a truly exhilarating experience of man vs. nature.

Spear fishing has progressed well beyond the use of a sharpened stick to the point that there are now countless types of spears and spear guns on the market made from all sorts of high-tech materials. In spite of the modern science employed in the development of that equipment, however, **successful spearfishing** still **depends on the fitness, abilities** and **endurance** of the fisherman.

Not only does advanced spearfishing require plenty of practice and the development of physical readiness, it is also a sport that demands patience and an in depth knowledge of the behavior of fish, the ability to read the conditions of the water and weather and an understanding of the indications or signs of good fishing spots.

That is not to say, however, that beginners can't enjoy the experience of spearfishing! There are many opportunities to participate in the sport in shallower waters, with experienced guides or good friends who have done it before or after taking some lessons. Spearfishing is a natural extension of snorkeling and freediving so many people get into the sport as a result of their participation in these other activities.

Just as in ages past, spearfishing can be a means to provide food for yourself and your family. It can be done to supplement the food budget or to ensure the highest quality and freshness of the catch. This is a highly sustainable form of fishing since there is no by-catch and only what will be used is taken from the environment.

Spearfishing has also become a competitive sport with countless enthusiasts pitting themselves against one another and the challenges of the ocean to come up with the largest fish in the shortest amount of time. There are plenty of thrills in the hunt for 'the big one' and great camaraderie among the participants.

*This book offers a look at various aspects of the sport of spearfishing:*

- from its rugged beginnings in the ancient and even relatively recent past

- as an exciting pursuit or a relaxing pastime

- as a skill that is enhanced with tips and suggestions from experienced spearos

- as a world-wide phenomenon with great places to enjoy exciting and spectacular spearfishing.

Come and discover the challenging and highly rewarding sport of spearfishing!

# CHAPTER 1 – WHAT IS SPEARFISHING?

## The Ancient Beginnings

**S**pearfishing is undoubtedly one of the oldest sports in the world. In ancient times, though, it was simply the means of survival for hunters who understood that a tool worked much more efficiently than bare hands. A sharpened stick could be thrown with great speed and accuracy, ensuring a good supply of fish for the family.

**Spears, harpoons and tridents** have been used for fishing or hunting in the marine environment for thousands of years. Their use has been recorded in cave paintings, biblical descriptions and by ancient historians from many different cultures. In many cases, the actual equipment has not changed much at all!

The catch in those days was limited to the distance a hunter could see and reach into the water. Later, a line was attached to hold the spear after it was thrown. Even then, access to fish and water mammals was minimal since hunting only took place from the relative safety of shore or a simple boat. Many superstitions and legends grew from the experiences of fishermen who tried to challenge deeper water for that elusive great catch.

# Newer Equipment

Spears and harpoons did not change much for countless millennia. Iron tips were added to harpoons in the 1700s and an **explosive harpoon gun** came along in the later 1800s. This type of large harpoon gun for whale hunting has been immortalized in stories such as *Moby Dick*. When elastic became available as a commercial product, it was used for personal **pole spears** and **Hawaiian slings** as a way to propel the shaft with more power than the human arm.

It was not until the 1940s and 1950s that significant changes were made to this basic fishing spear. At roughly the same time, based on the success of watertight swim goggles, came the modern forms of **diving masks, fins and snorkels**. A re-breather developed in the 1930s was proven to work quite well during WWII and became the basis for the sport of scuba diving. This technology allowed spear fishermen to stay under water longer and swim greater distances.

# Spearfishing Today

Modern technology has brought many changes to the equipment used for spearfishing but the main focus is still on the physical and mental ability of the fisherman. Whether for recreational or competition purposes, the hunter is required to match wits with the fish and overcome the obstacles presented by the ocean to catch and bring in the prize. Tournaments and the posting of record catches provide excitement and draw attention to the sport enticing more and more people to find out more about it. The fact that it is so environmentally friendly with no by-catch or habitat damage also appeals to a growing group of enthusiasts.

Spearfishing has become a **popular activity** both **as a relaxing sport** that provides fresh fish for dinner **and a competitive endeavor**. There are numerous clubs and organizations that promote spearfishing while helping to safeguard the environment and protect species that have become overfished. Laws limiting the size and number of fish that can be kept and restrictions on the use of powered spears and scuba gear help maintain the challenge of the hunt. In many locations, scuba tanks and pneumatic guns are completely outlawed.

Enthusiasts of spearfishing form a tightly knit community that support one another and promote the fun, excitement and allure of the sport. Safety and responsibility are strongly encouraged to ensure the sustainability of the sport for future generations and maintain the ecological balance of the oceans.

# CHAPTER 2 – METHODS OF SPEARFISHING

## No Diving

There are many cases where spearfishing is done from the shore, rocks or a small boat or pier **without** the hunter ever **getting in the water**. The presence of alligators, crocodiles or piranhas may prevent actual diving or swimming out to deeper water. For these reasons, many cultures have developed techniques for spearing fish, gigging them (with a multi-pronged tool instead of one with a single point) or bow fishing.

Even without these particular dangers, people may simply prefer to keep to the shallows and adjust their techniques accordingly. A good hunter can move in close to a fish in the water or take advantage of the pools formed among rocks. Elevated rocks also provide a better vantage point but taking the refraction of the image of the fish into consideration takes some practice. In time, understanding how to shoot makes this compensation natural and mechanical.

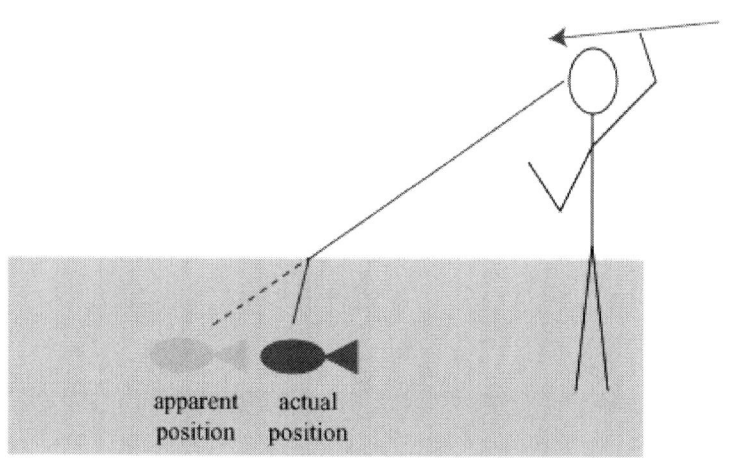

# Shore Diving

**H**istorically, spearfishing is most often practiced **under water** and **the beach is** the logical **point of access**. The diver enters the water and searches for fish, usually around ocean structures such as *rocks*, *reefs*, *sand bars* and *kelp beds*. From this starting point, it is common to reach depths of 5 to 25 meters (16 to 82 ft.) and even possible up to 40 meters (130 ft.) depending on the location of drop offs and the slope of the ocean floor.

Shore divers still need to be aware of the surroundings since sharks are common in tropical waters as they follow their food source and sub-tropical waters tend to have bigger waves that present a challenge to the stamina of the diver going in and out of the surf.

For added depth or a quicker descent the diver can jump into the ocean from a **headland** which is a **sheer drop right into the water**. Timing is highly important so that there is adequate depth and the diver does not get pushed back into the cliff by incoming waves.

Some fishermen assume that only *reef fish* can be caught while shore diving but there are also numerous *pelagic* (deep water) *fish* that can be found since they are attracted to the smaller fish nearer to shore as a source of food.

# Boat Diving

Many ocean structures lie offshore and are not accessible by shore diving. For that reason, boats can be used to take divers to a particular location where the boats can either troll or chum and wait for the spear fishermen to return with their catches or return later to retrieve divers.

Unlike the simple canoes and flat bottom craft that have been used for thousands of years, today's boat divers use all sorts of *motorized boats, kayaks* and even *personal watercraft*. Not only can the fishermen reach their favorite areas quickly and without over-doing it, they can more easily and safely save what they catch, take breaks between dives more comfortably and have transportation in the event of an emergency.

*Fish aggregating devices* (FADs) are commonly used sites for spearfishing since they attract up to 300 species of fish that like to hide and take advantage of the shadows. Oil rigs or other large platforms are relatively permanent structures but it is also possible to anchor buoys to large concrete blocks to create such an attraction. Using these man-made devices is ultimately simpler than swimming great distances looking for the traditional tell-tale signs of the presence of large numbers of fish – numerous birds and dolphins concentrated in a particular area.

# Blue Water Diving

**Extreme** is the best way to describe blue water spearfishing. This is a true test of stamina and skill since it involves **diving in the deep parts of the ocean** in the hunt for large pelagic game fish such as *tuna*, *marlin* and *Spanish mackerel*. A boat is used to take divers to a location where they most often enter the water and drift to locate fish. These divers take advantage of areas of up-welling that large fish use to swim among their food source.

*Disorientation is a major concern* for blue water spear fishermen because of the openness of the area and lack of reference points. This makes it difficult to judge distances, directions and even the size of the fish that are being targeted. In this case, the size of the eye of the fish helps the hunter gain perspective. With what may seem to be reverse logic, the smaller the eye in relation to the rest of the fish, the larger the fish.

Given the danger inherent in blue water diving, it is important to observe all the safety procedures associated with the sport. Knowing your limitations and not pushing too hard is necessary to help avoid accidents. It often takes more than one spear and a long swim to kill these pelagic fish and special breakaway rigs, larger guns and buoys and float lines are frequently used to provide assistance to the diver.

# Freshwater Spearfishing

Thousands of **lakes, springs, quarries** and **deep rivers** offer wonderful opportunities for freshwater spearfishing. Special attention needs to be given to these changeable environments but the challenges and rewards are just as exciting as in the open ocean.

**There are many** different **restrictions** related to freshwater spear-fishing around the world. In many countries, a license is required if spearfishing is not outright prohibited, only certain species and sizes of fish can be killed, night fishing and scuba are outlawed and no speared fish can be sold. Although it may seem quite restrictive, these rules are in place to ensure the survival of certain species and maintain the sustainability of the sport.

*In the United States regulations* for freshwater spear fishing are set by each individual state but the same general rules apply. *Licenses are mandatory and only rough fish* (non-game fish that have no real commercial value) *can legally be hunted* except for a few species limited to several states. State lands are restricted and swimming areas and conservation zones are also off limits.

Where it is allowed, diehard spear fishermen use scuba gear in the winter to **dive under the ice**. These climate conditions provide much better visibility since seasonal changes such as lake turn-over, flooding and algae blooms that significantly affect water quality and visibility are absent.

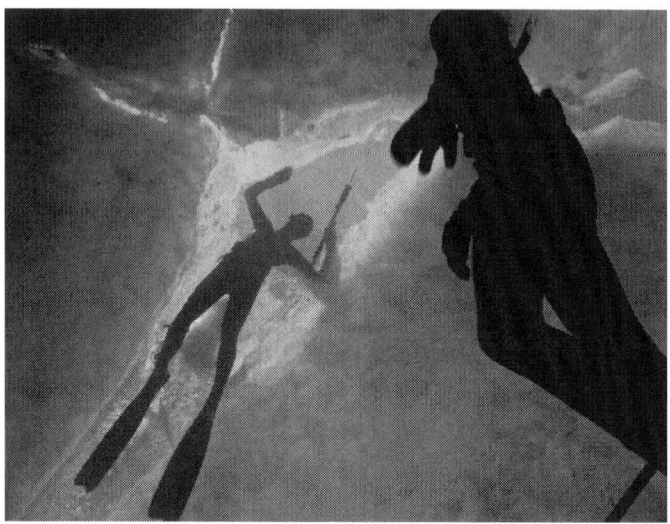

# Hole Diving

Whether you are in fresh or sea water, one great way to find fish is to locate **underwater holes and caves**. The fish feel more protected in semi-enclosed spaces and hide under ledges or in between large rocks or reef outcroppings. Different types of fish seek refuge in kelp beds and holes so it pays to know your target.

Light is very diffuse or even non-existent in some of these locations so it is important to have a light and keep you calm. It is easy to become disoriented when the darkness hides all traces of your path and that can be extremely dangerous. This is definitely a situation where diving with a partner or in a group pays off.

Another advantage of swimming with a partner while cave or hole diving is that one person can wait hiding in the recesses while the other person startles the fish in open water so they head for safety. This is similar to the technique of *'herding'* mentioned in the section on the *No Diving* method of spearfishing. It takes coordinated effort and careful monitoring of your air supply but can result in an amazing catch.

# Scuba Diving

**The use of scuba gear for spearfishing** is quite controversial. **In many locations** around the world, **it is illegal** to use any type of breathing apparatus so it is important to find out about any and all local laws and ordinances before going out.

Primarily, *scuba diving is the preferred method for spearfishing under ice, in caves and the extreme depths*. In other situations, it is counterproductive since the sounds made by the equipment and the release of bubbles with each breath tends to scare the fish making it very difficult to make any type of catch.

Choosing scuba breathing gear is determined by personal preference as well as the intended area and climate for diving and is beyond the scope of this book. Never the less, the essentials such as wetsuits, fins and masks are discussed in Chapter 5.

# CHAPTER 3 – PHYSICAL FITNESS AND PERSONAL PREPARATION

## Your Body

It can be said that virtually anyone who can swim can participate in spearfishing. While technically true, it is also a gross overstatement. Not only is swimming involved but when the excitement of the catch is added and the fish has to be retrieved and carried, there is much more strain on the body than is usually encountered during swimming.

The reality of spearfishing dictates that participants should be in **good**

**physical shape and have the ability to hold their breath for up to several minutes** at a time. No matter how good the equipment you carry may be, if you can't get to the fish and, more importantly, return to the surface, you will not succeed as a spear fisherman and could find yourself in real danger.

# Training For Success

Spearfishing can be just a simple matter of leisurely swimming around to find and catch fish. For the avid spearfishing enthusiast, though, a high degree of physical and mental preparation is needed for safety and success.

Even if you use scuba tanks to enable underwater breathing, body strength, general stamina and mental conditioning are important for any type of diving. You need to consider the extended length of time you may be in the water, the presence of rough seas or strong currents and the exertion of sprinting after a fish, shooting it and bringing it in.

There are actually several separate factors that contribute to the overall fitness required to become a competent, safe spear fisherman.

### 1. Strength

Strength is not only needed for swimming farther and faster, it is important for avoiding injury. By building up all the appropriate muscle groups, joints are better protected and overall function is improved. This type of strength training is not necessarily intended to increase muscle mass but does serve to generate greater efficiency of the neurological impulses between your brain and muscles.

### 2. Endurance

Even 'good' swimmers can improve their endurance to help become better prepared for spear-fishing. More than simply swimming more laps, the goal is to swim those laps using different combinations of strokes, different speeds and alternating distances to build up to more total distance with less need for rest periods.

### 3. Flexibility

For a smoother stroke that creates less turbulence as you swim and for more forceful contractions of elongated muscle fibers, flexibility training is beneficial to spear fishermen. Gentle yet progressive stretching of all muscles enhances flexibility, especially when the stretch is not rushed or bounced. The pull should be noticeable (but never hurt) and then held for more than 15 seconds – ideally up to two minutes! *Yoga* and *Pilates* are fantastic preparation for the rigors of spearfishing.

## 4. Controlled Breathing

Breathing is a natural function that is completely automatic, but when it comes to swimming, training your body to breathe efficiently is extremely important. This is especially true when free diving or engaging in deep blue water diving to spear 'the big one'. Relaxation is a major factor in controlled breathing and refers to a state of mind as well as all the muscles in the body including the face, head and neck.

## 5. Presence of Mind

Ultimately the most important safety factor involved in spearfishing aside from not shooting yourself or someone else is the ability to keep calm, relaxed and in control. Holding one's breath is quite unnatural and is something that requires practice and common sense. Panic is a sure way to end up in trouble so any technique that you can use to keep your composure under any circumstances is valuable. The ability to remain unruffled aids in the conservation of oxygen which can prolong your swimming range and time in the water.

# Choose What Works For You

There are countless 'experts' that have developed plans and programs for all sorts of physical training that can help you get in shape for spearfishing. Before pursuing any exercise or workout regimen, though, it is important to know that you are healthy enough to participate so consulting with a doctor and discussing your medical history is strongly recommended.

Considering the five factors that contribute to your overall readiness to challenge the deep, here are some suggestions that provide you with a place to start. Please note: this is **not** medical advice and all of the following information is simply intended to serve as basic guidelines.

# Strength Training

Improving the overall strength of your body **increases general functionality** and **allows** you to **swim more effectively**. That is crucial when you have to maximize your speed and distance due to the time restriction related to holding your breath. *The most effective strength training* for spearfishing is *accomplished through repetitions* and not necessarily by adding significant weight or resistance. Building muscle mass is not the goal but rather **improving the power to body weight ratio** by moving and lifting using light weights, resistance bands, medicine and Swiss balls or nothing more than the body's actual weight.

- Pull ups

- Bar dips

- Bridges

- 'Bicycling' on your back
- Abdominal crunches

- The Plank

- Kettle Bell Swing

- Stepping
- Lunges and Twists
- Rowing
- Squats

- Bear Crawling (on hands and feet – not knees)

- Pushups
  - With feet elevated
  - With one hand elevated

• Using weights and alternately lifting

• SEAL style

Wherever possible, mimicking the actual natural movements of the body provides a more effective workout than performing specific moves that target individual muscles. The neurological bonus of connecting and coordinating the movements and brain signals enhances your overall performance in that the efficiency of the body is increased and fatigue is reduced.

Convenience is the key to starting and maintaining any type of exercise routine and the fact that all of these activities can be performed at home makes it quite simple. It is important, though, to be sure that you are not straining with any of these exercises so initial instruction from a personal trainer or at a gym may be a good idea.

Just as with the stretching movements, your weight and resistance movements should be controlled and steady to avoid injury. Inhale before beginning any move so that you can exhale with the effort of performing the exercise. You inhale again as the effort is released or you are returning to the starting position.

# Endurance Training

In order to enjoy spearfishing and maximize your potential, you need to be comfortable achieving the distance you may be required to swim. For training purposes, **increase the distance you can swim comfortably before working to increase the speed** at which you are want to cover this distance.

This type of training involves longer and longer repetitions but the actual lengths and combinations are up to you. You should swim at a pace that allows you to keep your breathing under control and comfortable. When walking or jogging for exercise, the rule of thumb is to move at a pace that does not prevent you from carrying on a conversation. Your arms will undoubtedly become tired but this is part of the training and you will adapt quite quickly and build your muscle strength and endurance over time.

The idea is to perform repetitions based on distance at a speed which you find challenging but not really strenuous. In between the repetitions, take short periods of rest to quickly refresh and be ready to start again. The repetitions should not cover too great a distance that you become worn out because you do need to maintain your technique. Throughout this training, **the goal is to increase the number of repetitions and then the length of the distances all at a comfortable pace**. Eventually, you will cover longer distances and more repetitions with fewer and shorter recovery periods.

# Flexibility Training

**G**reater flexibility allows for economy of motion while swimming. This is **important for increased endurance and conservation of oxygen** for easy breathing during prolonged periods in the water. Additionally, full body flexibility is needed because *swimming* actually *uses almost every muscle in the body*, some obviously more than others, but all combine for controlled exertion that needs to be well coordinated.

- Shins

- Calf

- Quadriceps (front of thigh)

- Hamstrings (back of thigh)

- Hip Adductors (inner thigh)

- Glutes

- Latisimus Dorsi (the broad muscle of the back)

- Lower Back (extensors and flexors)

- Chest (pectorals)

- Core (abdominals and obliques)

- Shoulders (deltoids and trapezius)

- Triceps (the back of the upper arm)

**Stretching** is actually quite simple to incorporate into any exercise program. It can be done during the warm up or cool down associated with aerobic activities or strength training if it is not done as a separate workout routine.

There are many different basic stretches that can be performed after a simple warm up. A few **key points** to keep in mind **for these movements** are to:

1. Stretch slowly and smoothly as you inhale.

2. Stretch until you feel the pull but no pain.

3. Hold the stretch at least 10 to 30 seconds or more.

4. Never bounce during the stretch – relax while holding the position.

5. Release the stretch, relax and breathe deeply.

6. Repeat each stretch 2 or 3 more times.

**- Shins and Quadriceps**

- Hamstrings

- Hip Adductors

- Latisimus Dorsi and Back

- Chest and Shoulders

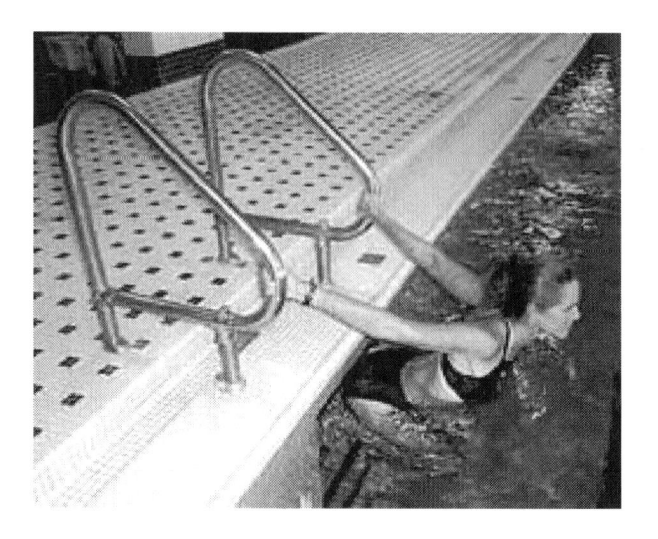

# Controlled Breathing Exercises

The body needs a steady oxygen supply to function properly. When using free diving techniques for spearfishing, the body is forced to adapt to both the lack of fresh oxygen and the effects of pressure that result in a slowing of the pulse and the constriction of blood vessels. These factors alter the way oxygen is used by the cells and the amount of air that is actually available at different depths.

***Aerobic exercise*** and ***yoga*** are fantastic ways to improve breathing in general and can be modified to create greater lung capacity. Deep breathing exercises force you to concentrate on your breathing technique and this also helps to relax you and lower your pulse rate. The more specific practices of ***hyperventilation***, ***breath holding*** and ***frog breathing*** are additional ways to build up your ability to function better with restricted air intake but should be done very carefully since pushing too hard can cause lightheadedness or fainting.

Professional instruction is recommended for anyone seriously interested in free diving because of the seriousness of the potential consequences. This kind of un-aided breathing involves the ability to hold the breath for extended periods under varying levels of exertion and is an integral part of the training undertaken by Navy Seals. In preparation for this type of instruction, here is an activity to help provide you with an idea of what your body experiences.

The *diaphragm* is the muscle that controls the expansion and contraction of the lungs. Like any muscle, it needs to be progressively challenged to improve its function. Throughout the **30 steps** that are considered a **workout**, you need to sit up straight but comfortably, breathe in and out as much, as hard and as long as possible without hurting yourself or blacking out, and be patient – improvement will occur slowly but steadily.

This **exercise** is physically really very simple although it can be mentally challenging. Slowly and consciously inhale as deeply as possible, trying to stretch it out over at least 5 seconds. Hold the breath until it begins to become uncomfortable and slowly exhale over at least 10 seconds. The general rule is to take twice as long to exhale as inhale. Be aware that you may feel as though blood is rushing to your head or you may even feel light headed. That is a normal reaction and indicates that you need to stop holding your breath! It is not really a timed activity – it is based on how you feel and how hard you are able to push yourself to extend the breath.

Practicing **deep breathing** twice a day is probably enough since you will undoubtedly be involved in other types of exercise and training to prepare for spear fishing that change the rate and depth of your breathing. **Never practice this technique in the water** since it is possible to pass out!

For even more intense training, devices known as **Air Restricting Devices** (ARDs) limit the amount of air flow on inhalations and exhalations so you have to work harder. Again, consult with a professional trainer and please use caution when practicing with this type of device!

# Developing Presence Of Mind

Stress is an ever-present element of life and spearfishing is a wonderful way to escape for a while and enjoy the benefits of swimming, the sun, fresh air and relative solitude. Spearfishing represents a means to relieve stress but it is critical to leave your stress far behind as you prepare to enter the water. **Peace of mind and** the **ability to remain calm** are necessary factors for a successful and safe experience since both affect the efficiency of your breathing and the conservation of energy.

As trite as it may sound, the best advice is to learn how to ***go with the flow***. Nature, especially water, is powerful so there is no benefit in fighting it, ignoring it or simply giving into it. Understanding how to work with your surroundings and taking advantage of all clues and circumstances enhances your own natural abilities in spite of being in such an alien environment. That is what is meant by going with the flow.

**Concentration** may seem to be contradictory advice after being told to 'go with the flow' but when you are well trained at focusing on your goal and being aware your surroundings, concentration is simply second nature and leaves the mind free to address any changes or obstacles that may arise. For the best performance, it is advisable to be clear about what you need to focus on, focusing only on things that you can control and remaining relaxed in the face of situations you can't control.

Just as you can train your muscles, you can also train your mind to focus and concentrate. **Simple exercises** taken from sports psychology **can help improve focus and the power of concentration** which in turn increase confidence and performance.

- Count backwards from one hundred
- Count backwards by threes – 100, 97, 94, 91, etc.
- Pick a word, sound or picture and think of nothing else

Each of these activities seems quite simple. You keep going until you are distracted or find your mind drifting. For most people, though, it is actually very difficult to get to the end of the task and it takes frequent practice to progress to the point where you can maintain the activity without losing focus.

# The Importance Of Proper Preparation

The most critical consideration for spear fishermen is the **ability to hold** their **breath** and maintain adequate oxygenation, especially when participating in blue water diving. There are complicated equations and explanations regarding the way the body uses the oxygen in the blood but the basic fact is that **it is extremely dangerous to participate in deep dives without training** and a thorough understanding of the effects of oxygen deprivation.

*Shallow-water blackout* is an unfortunately deadly possibility when freediving. It usually occurs within 15 feet (5m) of the surface because of the change in the water pressure and the resulting change in the body's physiology. At this point, the expanding lungs suck oxygen out of the blood and this can result in a swift loss of oxygen to the brain which causes the diver to pass out. If someone is not right there to see what is happening, death is usually the outcome.

Another aspect of proper preparation is the **understanding of the effects of cold on the body.** *Hypothermia* is also a deadly condition because it robs the ability to think clearly and make important decisions from the diver. Any time the body is in an environment that is cooler than body temperature physiological reactions take place to try to offset that difference. That is why the body shivers. As the cold persists, coordination is affected and muscle weakness sets in leading to confusion, drowsiness and apathy. In such an advanced situation, the diver needs to be handled quickly and with care, preferably by a medical professional.

Understanding and acknowledging your personal capabilities and limitations is the most important part of preparation for the extreme forms of spearfishing.

# CHAPTER 4 – HOW TO CHOOSE GUNS, TIPS AND SPEARS

## What is a spear gun?

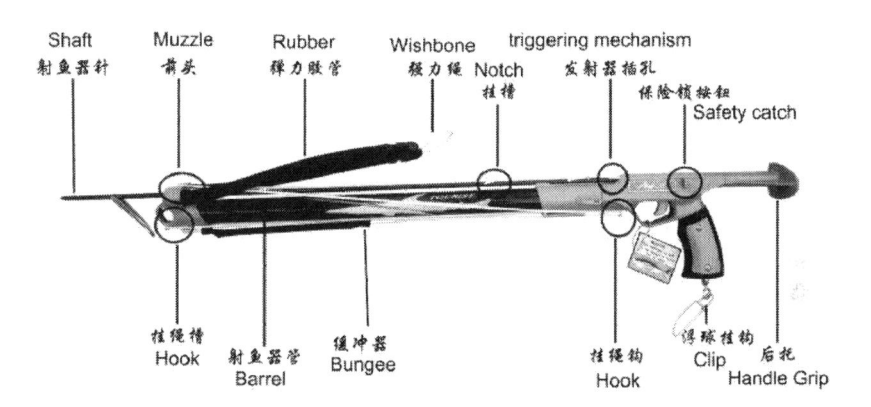

In the simplest terms, a **spear gun** is a tool that fires a spear at a fish underwater. That being said, though, there are almost as many different types of spear guns as there are fish to fire them at. Aside from the most basic pole spear, all spear guns are made of roughly the same parts.

**Barrel and Stock**

Since this is the body of the spear gun, it is *important to invest in a model that is strong and durable*. The barrel may be enclosed in the stock, actually be the stock or have a rail or groove that the shaft slides along when it is fired. The barrel can be made of a variety of materials including wood, graphite, aluminum, plastic and more. For more power, a barrel needs to be strong to hold the pressure of multiple bands but it is important to consider the weight of bigger guns. Longer guns tend to be able to shoot farther and provide more power.

**Muzzle**

At the very front of the gun, the muzzle holds the rubbers (bands) that propel the shaft from the gun. There are open and closed types, screw-in or loop bands and different materials such as nylon or aluminum. Open muzzles are quiet and allow for more stealth but closed muzzles are easier to load. Loop bands are a bit more difficult to change but don't break as readily as screw-in bands.

**Shaft**

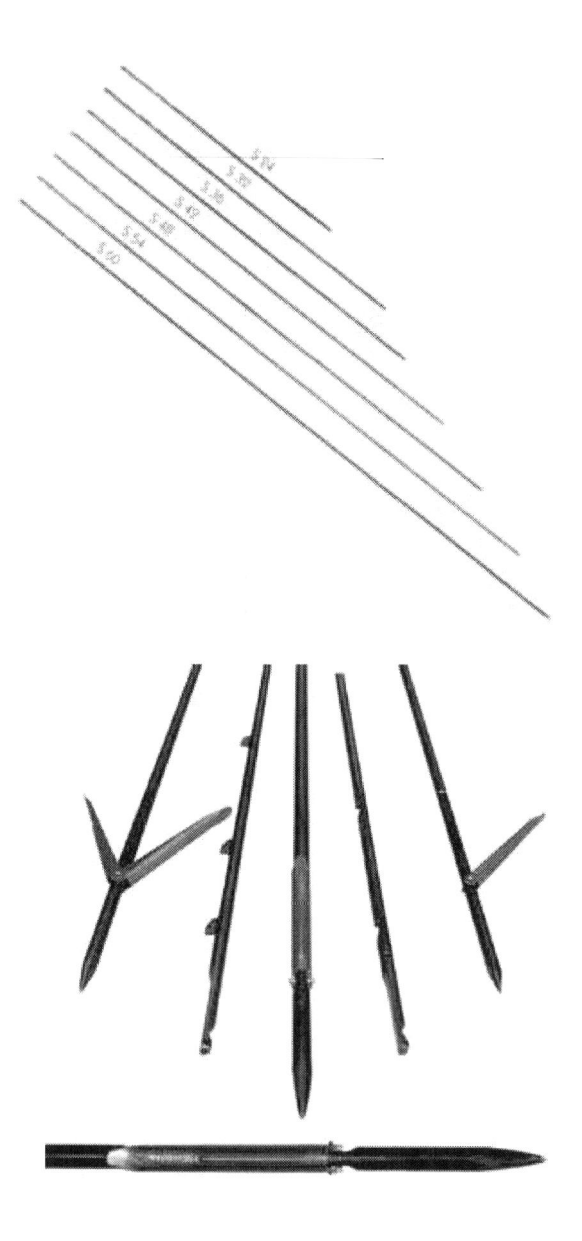

The shaft is actually the steel spear that shoots from the spear gun. There are many different lengths and thicknesses of shafts as well as degrees of flexibility, strength and spring depending on the size of the spear gun and the type of fish being hunted. It is important to have a good supply of shafts since they can relatively easily get lost or bent out of shape.

**Tip**

On the end of the shaft is a tip that pierces the fish like an arrow. A variety of types of tips are discussed later.

**Rubber (Band)**

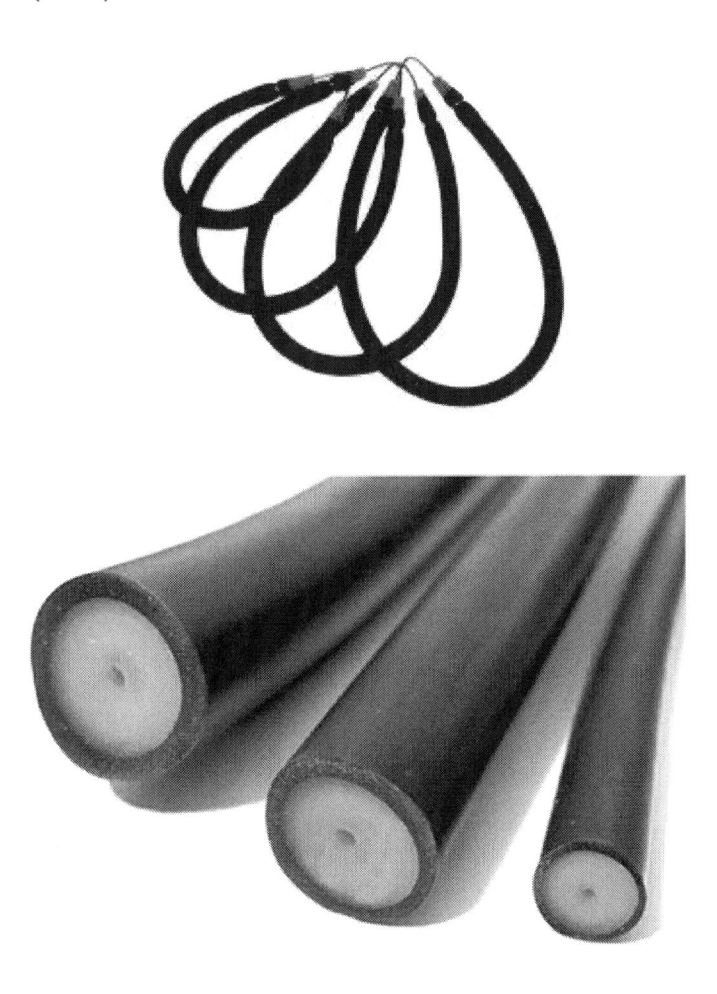

Except for pneumatic spear guns, bands are used to propel the spears. Bands come in different lengths according to the guns they fit and the power needed by the fisherman and can be used in multiples. Because of the direct relation of the band to the speed and power of the spear, it is important to use good quality products and to check your equipment frequently for wear or flaws.

**Wishbone (Bridle)**

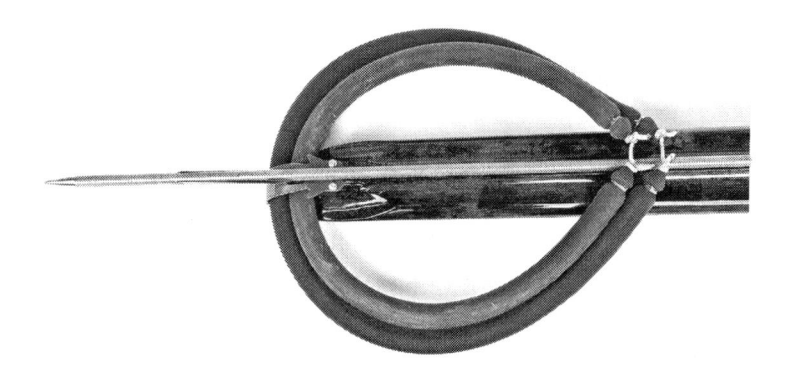

The wishbone connects the band to the shaft and can cause a lot of damage if it slips out of the notch and catches fingers during loading. Metal wishbones are strong and durable but a braided dyneema wishbone is much safer and does not lose much strength over time in comparison to metal models.

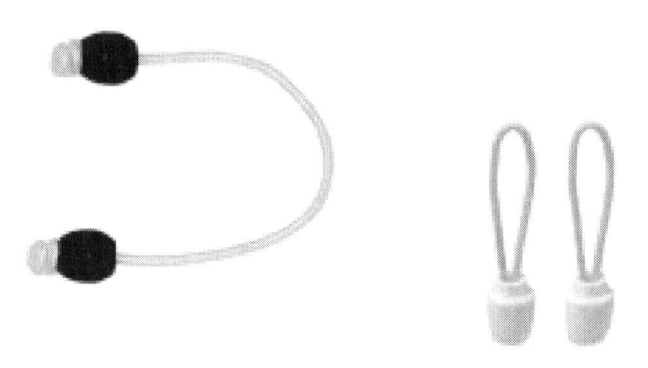

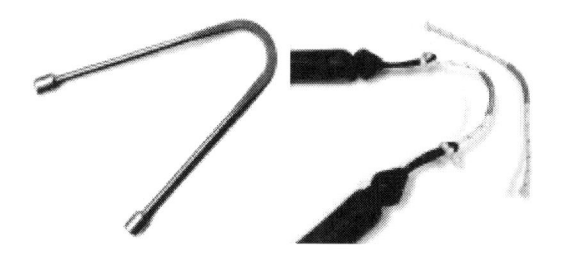

## Shooting Line

Cord, usually dyneema, which is attached to the shaft and the muzzle of the spear gun is called the shooting line. This keeps the gun and shaft connected so that the fisherman can retrieve the fish into which the shaft has embedded itself.

## Trigger

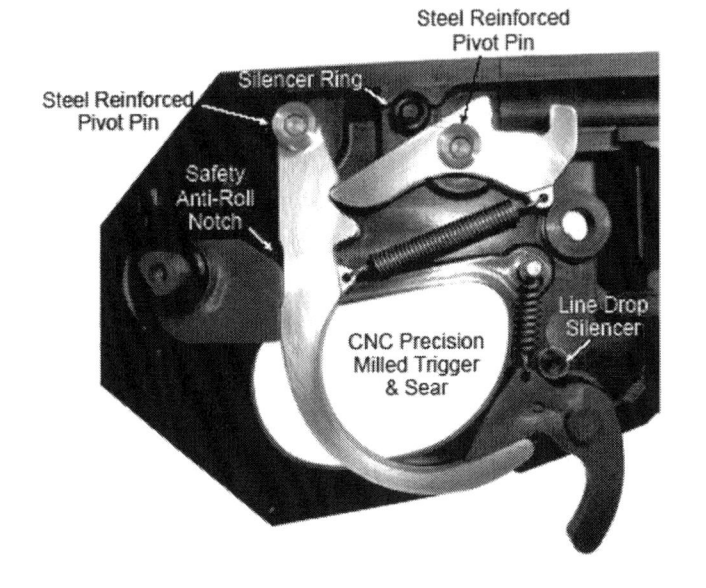

Steel Reinforced Pivot Pin
Silencer Ring
Steel Reinforced Pivot Pin
Safety Anti-Roll Notch
CNC Precision Milled Trigger & Sear
Line Drop Silencer

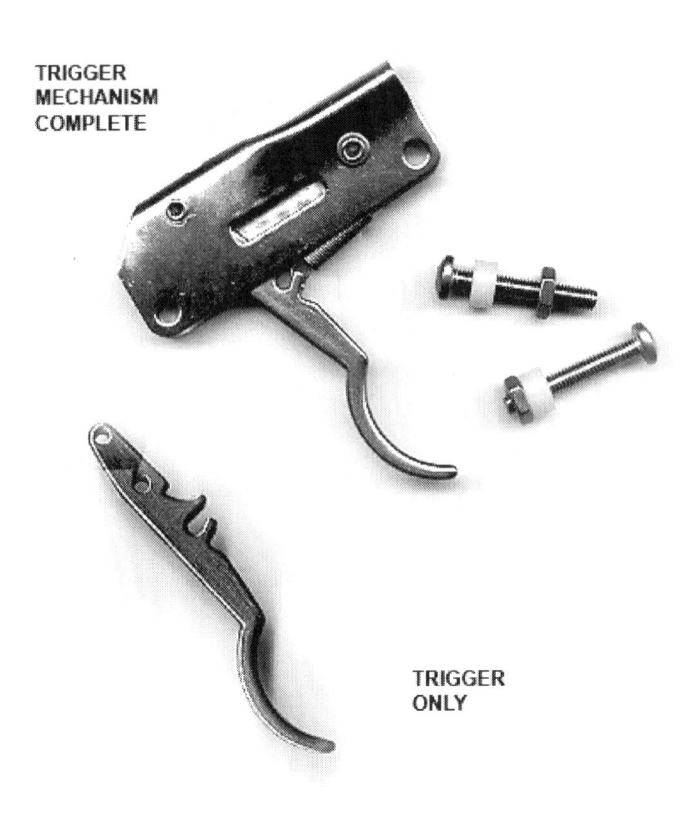

TRIGGER MECHANISM COMPLETE

TRIGGER ONLY

The trigger mechanism is the most complicated part of a spear gun since it needs to be powerful enough to propel the shaft yet function smoothly and quietly. A variety of mechanisms are available that differ in the way they operate, the make-up of the inner workings and the overall design, not to mention price.

**Loading Pad**

At the very back of the spear gun, the loading pad is actually the butt of the gun or it can also be a detachable unit. It is cushioned and designed to provide a bit of protection to the fisherman during the loading of the spear gun. The amount of pressure needed to pull the bands to load the spear gun can injure a person so the loading pad is used on larger guns to reduce the chance of bruising or injury.

# Selecting The Right Gun For Your Needs

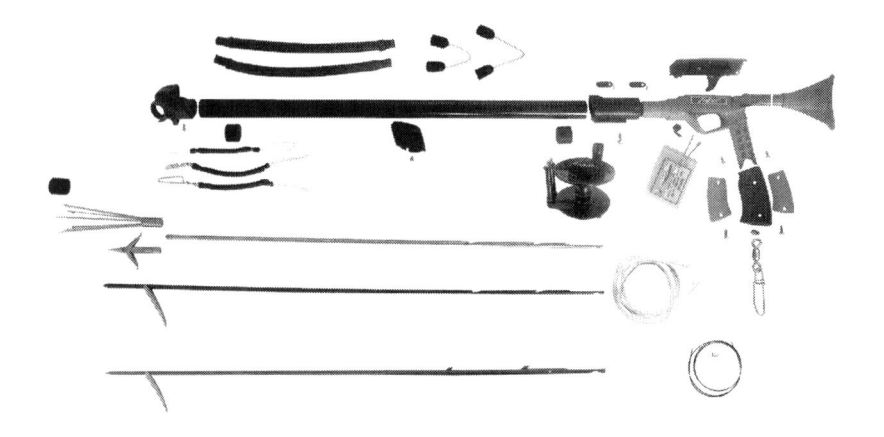

There are **only a few things to consider** when choosing the right spear gun for your activities: *size, noise* and *price*.

**The size of the gun** depends more on the conditions of visibility than anything else. The clearer the water, the longer the gun you will need because you will be firing from a greater distance. Cloudy water or close quarters such as in a cave, around a wreck or among rocks makes the use of a shorter gun more efficient.

The **action of the gun** as well as the **trigger mechanism needs to be quiet** so as not to alert the fish to your presence and scare them off.

**Price**, like with so many things, is relative and a higher price does not necessarily guarantee better success as a spear fisherman.

All spear guns are broken down into two basic categories: *pneumatic* and *band powered guns*.

**Pneumatic guns** reached the height of their popularity in the 1960s and 1970s although they still enjoy limited use with some spear fishermen due to their tremendous strength and minimal recoil. They are generally considered to be difficult to load, much more difficult to maintain and can be impractical for the casual spear fisherman to use.

**Band powered guns** on the other hand can also be quite powerful, are virtually silent, easier to aim and require little maintenance. It is extremely simple to adjust the strength of the gun by adding more bands and plenty of sizes are available to handle any target fish.

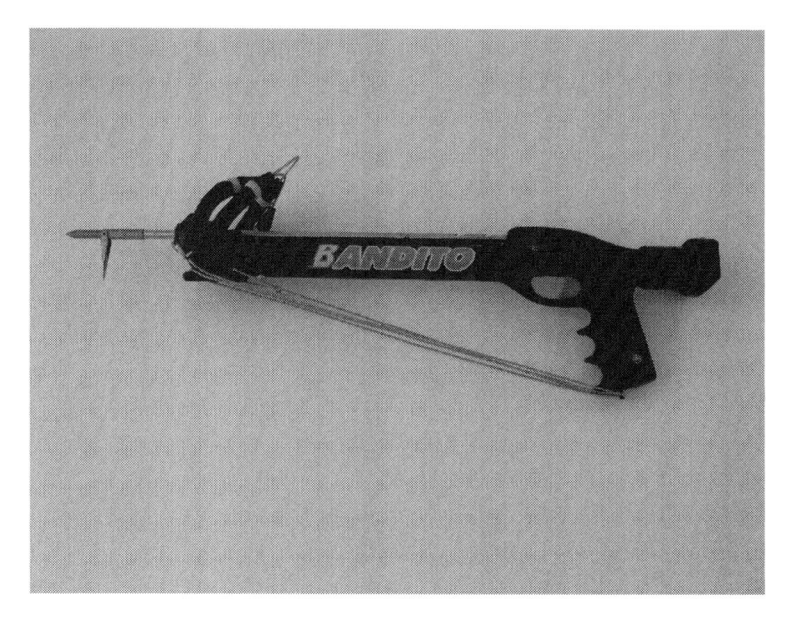

All of the various models of spear guns have advantages and disadvantages depending on individual needs and tastes. Many styles of trigger mechanisms, grips, barrel and shaft materials and loading configurations as well as sizes and shaft thicknesses and lengths cater to personal preferences.

*Apnea, Beuchat, Cressi, JBL International, KOAH, Mares, Nemrod* and *Riffe* are just some of the top names of speargun manufacturers that supply all different types of equipment for spear fishermen – form the beginner to the expert.

# Categories Of Spearfishing Spears And Guns

For most spearfishing activities, the common equipment may be a pole spear, a Hawaiian Sling or a spear gun with a trigger mechanism. Pneumatic or air powered guns have become more efficient and are increasingly gaining in popularity again in spite of the perception of them being harder to maintain. Traditionally, guns powered by elastic bands are used to provide more power than is possible by simply throwing the spear by hand.

**Pole Spear**

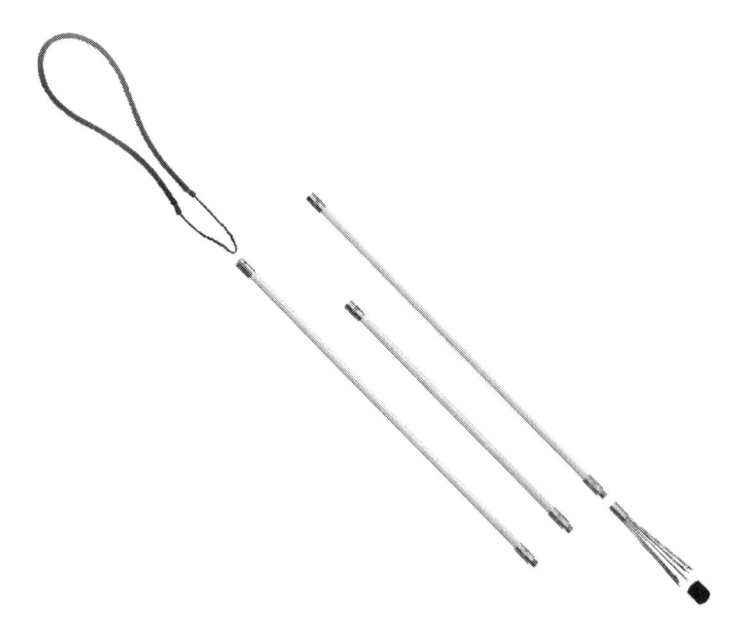

A small step up from simply throwing a spear at a fish, a pole spear is powered by an elastic band attached to the spear and stretched to provide thrust. This is the most basic equipment.

## Hawaiian Sling

A step up from the pole spear, the Hawaiian Sling works on the principle similar to that of a bow and arrow. The spear shaft passes through a hole in a handle and is pulled back against the attached elastic band which propels it when released.

## Euro Guns

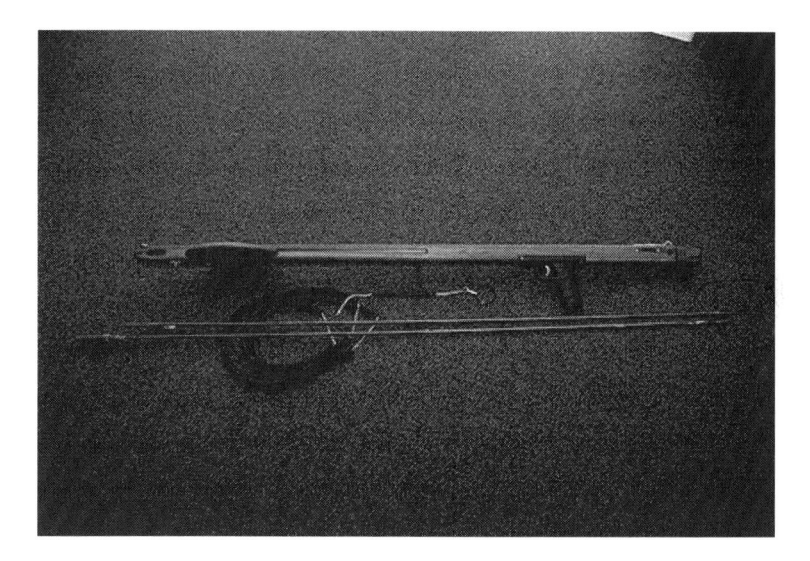

These guns were designed for European spear fishing where the goal is to hunt smaller fish. Euro-band guns are smaller than traditional guns and are fast and accurate.

## Rail Guns

A rail gun, also known as a South African band gun, is a variation on a euro-band gun with a thicker spear and a rail for added support since the fish hunted in South Africa are bigger than those hunted in Europe.

## Multiple Band Wooden Guns

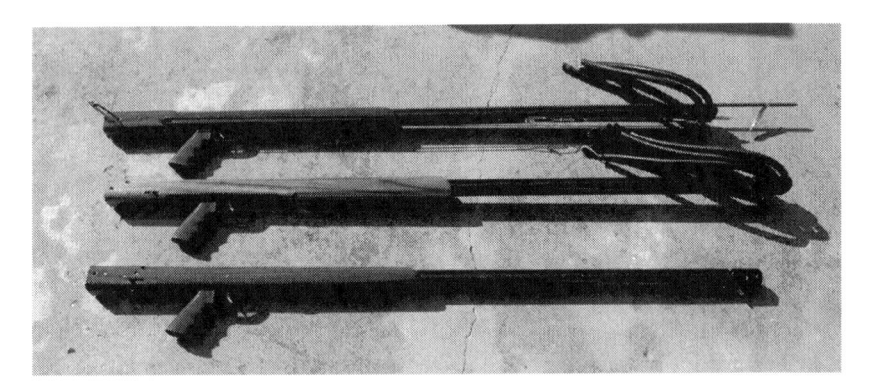

Extended firing range and greater power are the benefits of heavier-duty wooden guns that can hold up to 8 or more bands. The strength of the wood prevents barrel flex that distorts aim but these guns are heavier and produce strong recoil.

## Hybrid Guns

Hybrid guns use the strength of the wooden stock and a titanium or carbon fiber barrel with the shorter barrel length of the Euro-band gun.

Generally speaking, the clearer the water and the greater the visibility, the longer the spear gun should be. For example, with visibility up to 50 feet

(15 m) a **euro** or **rail gun** should be about 52 inches (130 cm) and a **wooden gun** should be about 63 inches (160 cm).

For reef diving, the numbers drop only slightly but for kelp or cave and hole diving where the visibility is greatly reduced, the length of the **euro** or **rail gun** should only be about 24 to 28 inches (60 – 70 cm) and the **wooden gun** 44 to 50 inches (110 - 127cm). This takes reduced maneuverability and space into account.

# The Choices Of Spear Tips

Tips that mount on the head of the spear shaft come in several styles, sizes and shapes and their choice depends on the kind of spear fishing that is being planned. Plenty of versatility is provided by the interchangeable nature of many of these tips.

**Cluster Tips**

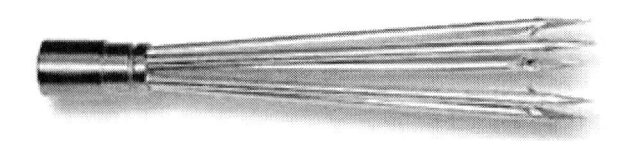

Cluster tips consist of prongs with barbs on the end that point outwards. These are ***most effective for smaller reef fish***  because the prongs provide a greater striking area. A cluster tip is also commonly used in hand spears.

**Harpoon**

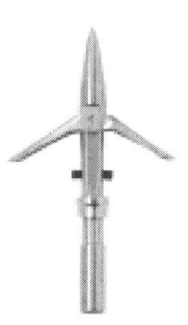

This single point is streamlined and usually comes with one or two flappers which prevent the spear from coming out of the fish. There is little resistance so this is a fast tip that ***works for both small and large fish***.

**Trident Head Tips**

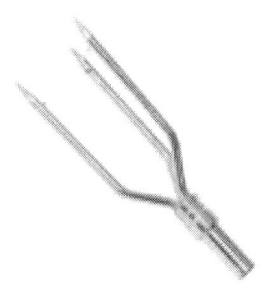

*Used for smaller fish*, the trident resembles a pitchfork with 3 or 5 prongs that form a straight line. Similarly, a *paralyzer tip* has three prongs which are set in a triangular formation and used primarily on pole spears.

**Barbed Tips**

Barbs are *common on* virtually *all tips* since they help to anchor the tip in the fish so it can't get away. The barbs also provide greater accuracy since they act like fins and stabilize the spear as it moves through the water.

**Slip Tips**

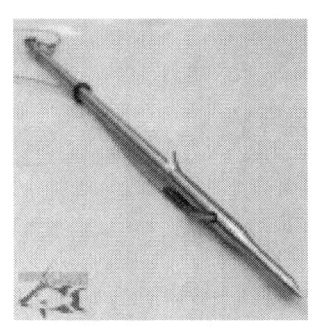

For use when hunting the *larger species of fish*, a slip tip is a long, hard point that can pierce through even the bones of the big fish. Moldings help guide the spear so that it is also effective at longer distances as long as the shooter compensates for the fall of the spear due to the extra weight of the tip.

**Breakaway Tips**

*Larger fish* can take a long time to wear out so you can bring them in. When hunting these species, it is best to use breakaway tips. Another use of breakaway tips is around rocks and reefs. They separate from the shaft to minimize damage and prolong the useful life of the shafts.

# CHAPTER 5 – OTHER EQUIPMENT FOR BETTER SPEARFISHING

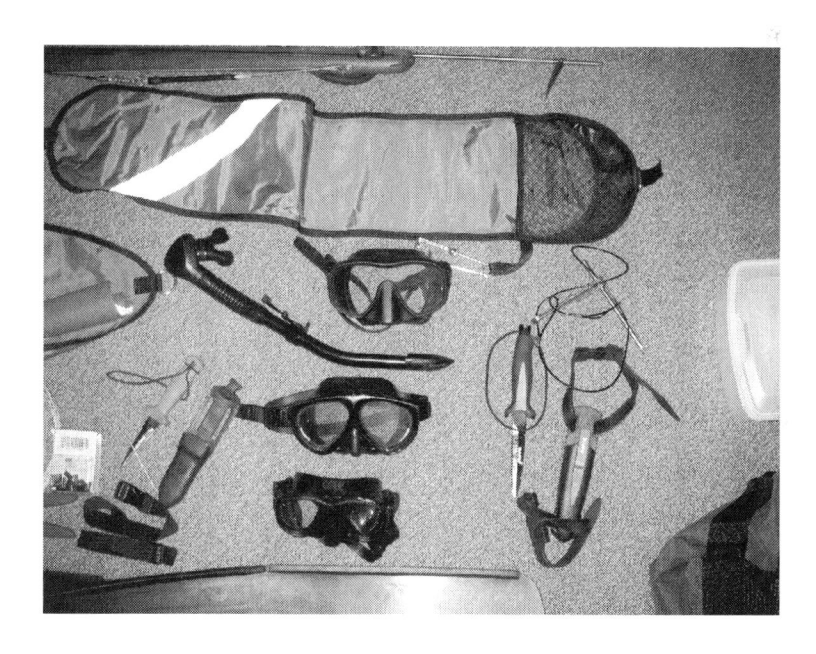

## The Basics

As with almost any other sport, you can enjoy spearfishing with a bare minimum of equipment. A bathing suit and your spear gun are all you really need but certain other pieces of gear make the experience easier and much more enjoyable. Of course, you can also go to the extreme and invest a lot of money in all sorts of gizmos and gadgets but they don't necessarily increase your success or pleasure.

***The most important pieces of equipment*** to purchase to help with spearfishing ***are masks, fins and snorkels***. Obviously, masks allow you to see much more efficiently under water and fins add significant strength and range to your swimming ability. Snorkels allow you to swim with your face submerged so it is easier to spot fish and you create less of a disturbance to the surface of the water.

**Masks**

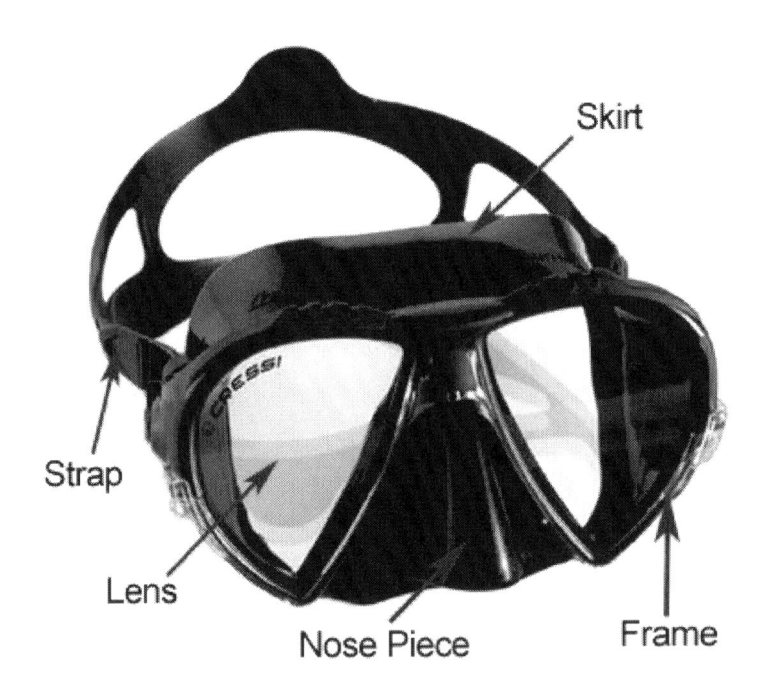

For something that appears so simple, **choosing a mask** requires plenty of patience and some expert advice. Not only does the mask serve as a way to see what is around you but it also affects the amount of air you can hold. It needs to fit perfectly so there are no leaks, no pinching and no fogging. In fact, selecting the right mask is all about function, not fashion.

The most common misconception is that it is OK to use a **scuba mask** for spearfishing. It can be done but scuba masks tend to be too large with too much air volume needed to equalize pressure. Unlike scuba diving that inherently provides plenty of oxygen to the diver through the air tank, freedive spearfishing requires holding your breath for long periods. A spear fisherman cannot afford to 'waste' oxygen on clearing a large mask so low volume masks are definitely preferable.

**Facial shape is the most important determiner** for selecting a diving mask for spearfishing. The mask has to comfortably accommodate your facial features including facial hair to be as effective as it can be. You begin the selection process by holding a mask gently up to your face with both hands using your thumbs to hold back the skirt slightly. When you feel the mask, release your thumbs. Without applying any extra pressure, hold the mask in place and check around the edges for any sign of light showing between your face and the skirt.

If there is no visible light and the mask seems to hold in place with almost no pressure, you are off to a good start! Next, inhale gently and see if the mask does stay on your face without a big breath or using your hands. For men, being clean-shaven is important so there is silicone to skin contact.

The final check for **appropriate fit** is to press the mask firmly against your face using both hands applying pressure to the entire frame of the mask. If there are any spots that hit your lips, nose, eyebrows or cheekbones, you may need to find another mask. What may feel like a little bit of pressure on land can feel like a vice under water so there should be as little contact between the glass or hard frame of the mask and your face as possible.

Once you are assured of a comfortable fit, you can consider options such as *mirrored* **or** *tinted lenses*. Darkening the lens helps in certain situations but can be detrimental if you intend to dive in caves or when there is poor visibility. Certain tints help increase depth perception and clarity but others can distort vision. Black silicone masks are considered to be the best but clear silicone provides more of a feeling of openness as do side windows. However, these windows increase mask size and lead to a high-volume.

**Fins**

Every diver you ask will have a different answer about the 'right' kind of fins to use for spearfishing. There are countless brands and models on the market so experience is the best determining factor. The general consensus is that *closed-foot design fins* **are the best choice for free diving and spearfishing**. Worn with neoprene socks, they should have a solid foot pocket without straps that fit to hold your feet comfortably. Different brands have foot pockets with different shapes and dimensions so it is important to try a variety and find the one that best matches your feet, provides stability and maintains comfort. *Open-heeled fins* allow for adjusting the size but do not provide the power you can get with closed-heel fins so sharing fins with other divers is probably not a good idea. If the fins are too tight, your feet may cramp but if they are too loose, they will rub your feet and give you blisters or simply fall off.

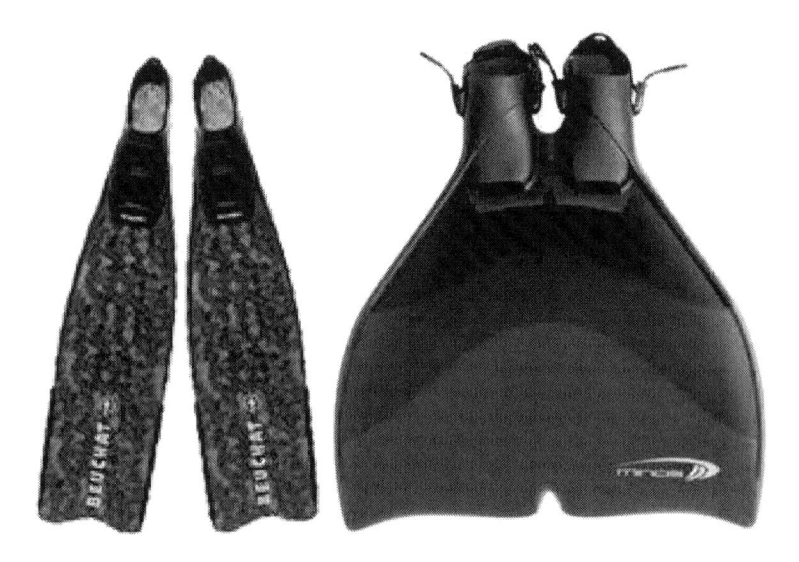

A basic fin with a conventional design is the best way to start if you have never used fins for swimming. From there, it is easy to experiment with other models that have been designed to minimize water turbulence, enhance the power of each kick or improve agility and the ability to pivot.

*The blades* for spearfishing fins **should be about a meter long** and not be too stiff. Plastic can be rigid and frequently does not provide enough 'give' so some divers automatically choose a fiberglass/carbon composite blade. The ultimate selection is made according to your weight. A stiffer blade is intended for a heavier diver or those who want to achieve greater depths. There are also various shapes and widths available so renting different fins is one way to figure out what feels right and works best for you.

**Snorkels**

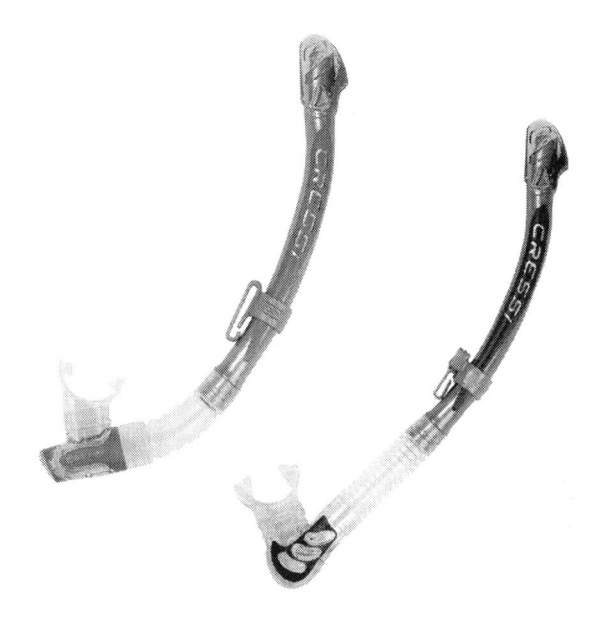

Unlike masks and fins, snorkels are easy to find and can be quite basic. **The most important consideration is comfort** since you don't want hard plastic pressing into your tongue or gums that could lead to blisters or bleeding. Avoid caps, purge valves and anti-splash components because they don't really help and can actually create unneeded drag.

# And Beyond...

Other types of equipment are quite helpful if not actually important for successful spearfishing adventures. Safety is always the primary concern for anyone in the water so anything that can preserve the body's energy, integrity and flotation could mean the difference between a good time and a disaster.

**Knives**

For the purposes of spearfishing, a small, simple knife should be adequate to cut away line or seaweed in the event of becoming entangled. The knife should fit into a sheath that can be worn on the arm or leg and be easy to access. If there is a greater possibility of attracting sharks, a larger knife may be considered but weight and added bulk can reduce dive time and affect the quality of a swim. Find the smallest knife that can get the job done effectively.

**Socks and gloves**

Neoprene socks have already been mentioned in connection with diving fins. They help improve the fit of the fins, prevent blisters and provide warmth. Gloves also serve to keep the hands warmer but they also provide protection from rope burns or cuts from fish gills, spines or teeth. Plain cotton gloves are usually enough but heavier leather-palmed gloves allow you to maintain sensitivity while covering the tops of the hands.

**Stringers or mesh bags**

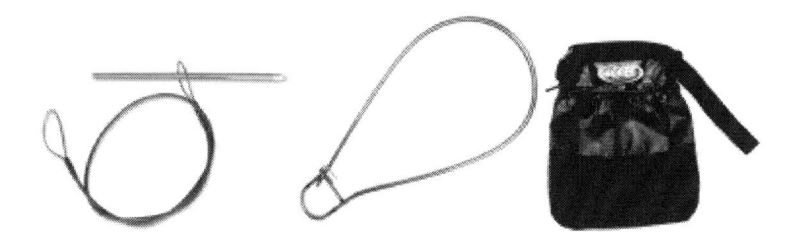

Since the goal of spearfishing is to catch fish, a stringer or bag should be used to hold onto the prize. A stringer can be attached to the diver's float line or secured around the waist, although carrying around dead fish could lure predators. The sharp point of a stringer can be used as an iki jime spike to finish off a speared fish that has not died but it can't necessarily replace a knife for other situations.

**Weight belts**

Depending on where you intend to fish and your overall strength and ability, a **weight belt can help overcome the natural buoyancy of the body**, especially if you are wearing a wet suit. Wearing weights helps you get to the bottom quicker and allows you to lie in wait without feathering your hands or feet to maintain your position but it also acts as an anchor that could prevent you from returning to the surface without extra effort. It is important to only use a weight belt with a quick release buckle to prevent a serious accident. Using weights is something that should be done only after you have some experience diving and with the advice of others who know what they are doing.

There are a **number of factors to consider when choosing weights** – your own weight and body fat index, the thickness of a wet suit, salt or fresh water, the depth you plan to dive to, water temperature and the mathematics of positive/negative buoyancy. This means that the body will float, sink or maintain position. It is also affected by holding a breath and releasing it. Most men can use a minimum of 3 to 6 pounds (1 ½ - 3 kg). With a wetsuit, at least 8 pounds (3 ½ kg) may be needed to begin with. Some divers use extra weights to drop quickly to a certain point then remove those weights and attach them to a floatline.

The best way to determine the appropriate weight is to strap on the minimum weight, dive to a depth of 30 feet (9 m) and see if you float back up to the surface. If you do, add more weight until you can maintain that depth. It is always better to be under-weighted so there is less likelihood of a problem re-surfacing.

**Float lines and buoys**

Even if marking your location with a buoy is not required by local law, it is an excellent idea so that other swimmers, divers and especially boaters know to keep clear. For your purposes as a spear fisherman, though, a buoy with a float line attached to your spear gun is a way to tire out a large fish and then transport all your catch home. There are many different buoys but they should fly either the international red and white flag accepted in the US or the blue and white 'alpha' flag to indicate the presence of divers under water. As for the line, yellow or white lines are considered high visibility under water. For more stealth, red, black and blue lines disappear from view.

## Wetsuits

Not only do wetsuits serve to keep a spear fisherman warm, they offer protection from cuts and abrasions that may be caused by scraping along the bottom, encountering rocks or coral or being side-swiped by fish. There are many styles from full-body suits with hoods to those with short sleeves and short legs and different thicknesses for varying degrees of warmth. Commonly black, wetsuits also come in a variety of camouflage patterns and colors. Wetsuits that are made specifically for spearfishing offer padding on the knees, elbows and chest to provide some cushioning and to aid in loading the gun.

For the least thermal protection, *'skins'* or *lycra suits* provide a thin layer of protection from the sun, rubbing against rough surfaces and stings. **Open cell neoprene wetsuits** are relatively soft and flexible allowing for efficient insulation and a wide range of motion. These suits tend to be fairly expensive and tend to be damaged easily but are considered to be the best option. **Closed cell neoprene wetsuits** are more durable and less expensive than open cell neoprene suits but can be restrictive and abrasive to wear and are more difficult to put on and take off.

Thermal protection for **warm**, **moderate** and **cold** water depends on the thickness of the material, usually 1 to 1.5 mm, 3 to 5 mm and 7 mm or more. Some suits improve both insulating ability and movement by using different thicknesses such as 5mm in the torso but less in the extremities and even less around the joints. Just as in dressing for any outdoor elements, each person is different and what is 'enough' for one may not do much of anything for someone else.

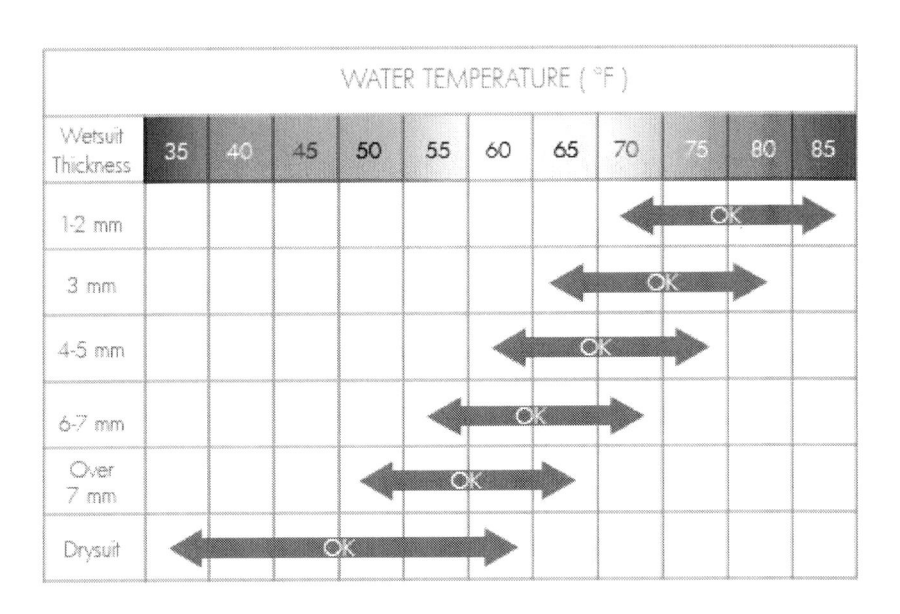

| Wetsuit Thickness | 35 | 40 | 45 | 50 | 55 | 60 | 65 | 70 | 75 | 80 | 85 |
|---|---|---|---|---|---|---|---|---|---|---|---|
| 1-2 mm | | | | | | | | ← | OK | → | |
| 3 mm | | | | | | | ← | OK | → | | |
| 4-5 mm | | | | | ← | OK | → | | | | |
| 6-7 mm | | | | ← | OK | → | | | | | |
| Over 7 mm | | | ← | OK | → | | | | | | |
| Drysuit | ← | OK | → | | | | | | | | |

WATER TEMPERATURE (°F)

# And Then Some...

Although not advisable for most divers, one final piece of equipment to bring along when fishing in tropical waters with the likely appearance of sharks is a **bang stick**. This is considered a firearm and can be quite dangerous if used improperly but is comforting to have in the event of sharks becoming attracted to your motion or that of the fish you are hunting. It is possible to use 'blank' rounds to frighten off predators and thereby reduce the risk of serious injury to yourself or other divers.

While it is important to be aware of sharks and monitor their action, most divers will not have to worry about a dangerous encounter. Sharks are curious and may investigate a diver but not stay around.

### *The best advice for divers in this situation is*:

- Keep calm and stay close to a buddy

- Keep away from sharks – never act aggressively

- Move slowly and gently and stay near the bottom

- Stand your ground or swim toward the shark – your larger presence will intimidate it

- String your catch to a float line so it is not on your body

In areas where it is not illegal to spearfish at night or for following fish into a cave, a good dive light (**underwater waterproof flashlight**) makes it easy to see. They also provide a way to signal other divers. These can be found at dive shops as well as on line in a range of prices from $10 to $100.

# CHAPTER 6 – TECHNIQUES AND TIPS FOR SPEARFISHING

## What You Need To Know Before Hitting The Water

**S**pearfishing is supposed to be fun and it can be with just a bit of caution and common sense. Physical fitness has been covered well in Chapter 3 but it is worth repeating here. Spearfishing involves a tremendous expenditure of energy in the water and can be dangerous in the event of a medical emergency. *It is important to know your capabilities and limits and only perform as much as common sense allows*.

**Using the proper gear is** also **a key element to** successful, enjoyable **spearfishing** so getting and following good advice provided by experienced spear fishermen is crucial. Additionally, it is a good idea to be completely familiar with all the equipment you plan to use before heading out to the deeps. Troubleshooting and having an idea about what to do if something goes wrong is also a good exercise and can save valuable time and prevent panic out in the water.

**Experiment with buoyancy** and wearing a weight belt or vest before actually going spearfishing. Get used to swimming with the equipment you plan on carrying and develop a feel for the weight, flotation, recoil and pull of the spear gun and line. Part of this process of acclimation is the awareness of the physiological effects of depth on the body in relation to its use of oxygen. Remember, when swimming to significant depths, less oxygen will be available to your body as you rise to the surface and it is quite possible to black out before reaching the surface. (This is called *shallow-water black out* and is quite common. See Chapter 3).

Before any spearfishing trip, **make sure that you know** what **the local laws** are governing the types of fish that can be hunted, the sizes of those fish that are allowed and any other restrictions that may pertain to equipment and methods of spearfishing. Take the time to find out about the underwater environment and currents or go with an experienced diver familiar with the locale the first time in a new spot. This will minimize your risks and provide you with an advantage for finding fish where you might not expect to.

# Spearfishing Is A Science And An Art

Although many spearos may try and tell you there are tricks to having a great catch, **the most important advice is to relax and enjoy the experience**. With more and more practice and exposure to different environments, you will soon discover how much fun the sport is – you won't have to concentrate so much on your breathing and general technique.

Over time, the real beauty of the sea will open itself to your full appreciation and you will join the thousands of others who have developed an abiding respect for the richness and diversity it offers.

Successful spearfishing is supposed to be fun but it is not about simply swimming around firing off your spear gun. There are tried and true techniques for catching great fish and the key is to understand fish behavior and the conditions of the sea. You will learn the indications of good hunting grounds and the best ways to approach your targets.

# Common Approaches To Catching Fish

Different species of fish respond to spearos in a variety of ways – fear, curiosity and aggression. For that reason, it is important to understand the habits of the fish you are trying to catch as well as others native to the area and practice a number of **different techniques for the best approach**.

1. Swim slowly and gently with your arm extended only half way out as you survey an area. Lots of kicking and splashing not only scare away the fish, it can also attract sharks. Blending in with the environment is the number one key to successful spearfishing.

2. Don't waste time following small fish! There are plenty of fish in the sea so take your time and get a good look around before shooting the first thing you see. Use your free hand to pull yourself along the bottom.

3. Waiting, although using up oxygen, is also important so that the fish are not spooked by your presence. This can be done from the surface (and is great with a snorkel) or on the bottom after a quick dive. Never swim or wait in the middle depths because you present an unusual element in the environment which scares the fish.

4. Keep track of underwater hiding places. Make a mental note of ledges,

holes, rock fields, submerged structures and other features that offer protection to fish.

5. Use weights to carry you to the bottom to reduce the amount of motion you perform. This not only helps you to conserve energy and oxygen, it also minimizes vibrations created by the motion of your fins that alert the fish to the presence of an intruder.

6. Fish are naturally curious so many will investigate something new in the environment. This only works when you move very slowly or can remain still. This is simple when you take advantage of natural camouflage or even stir up sand to cloud the water.

7. Carry small shells, rocks or pieces of coral to rub together or tap. These vibrations draw in inquisitive fish and bring them into spear gun range. This can also be done at the surface well away from your boat by tapping a knife against your spear gun.

8. When you spot a good target from the surface, take a deep breath and dive down directly on top of the fish and extend your arm fully to take a shot. This is the best way to remain unseen by the fish and it provides a good opportunity to get close enough for a sure hit but not closer than 20 inches (50 cm). If you get any closer, the shaft will not have the opportunity to gain enough velocity for a strong hit. Learning to judge distances underwater is important because the range of most spear guns is limited to 10 – 12 feet (3 to 4 m).

9. Chumming with a fish's natural food source such as mussels, smaller fish or sea weed is sometimes done to attract targets.

10. Aim for the area right behind the gills, toward the upper body. Damaging the spine is the best way to reduce the fight a fish will put up.

11. Once a fish is speared, get to it as quickly as possible and put it in a bag to minimize the chance of losing it as you remove the spear. If the spear did not finish it off, use an iki jime or knife to prevent too much thrashing around. This could cause the fish to come off the tip or attract unwanted attention from predators.

Unlike rod fishing which seems to be done best in overcast and rainy conditions, spearfishing depends on good visibility. You need the sun to reach through the water so you can spot fish and no raindrops or wind to disturb the surface. A rising or high tide can be helpful by bringing nutrients into the area and fishing in the early morning takes advantage of the time when fish are likely to be the most active.

No matter which approach you use to hunt for and catch fish, always remember to watch out for your depth, available air supply, the distance to your boat or the shore and your body heat. Remember – the most important tip for successful spearfishing is to focus on safety first.

# Situations To Avoid

**O**ne of the most important unwritten rules of spearfishing is to **shoot only what you intend to eat**. That means that waiting for the largest fish instead of shooting small fish is a better choice. There is no such thing as 'catch and release' with spearfishing so you have to be sure you can identify the species and size of the fish you are aiming at before you kill it.

**If you miss your target, retrieve your shaft**. That is easiest when there is a line attached to the shaft with or without a reel. Leaving a shaft with a tip is a danger to wildlife and other spearos and swimmers. Missing the target is also a serious issue when you are diving around other people or among coral reefs. It is important to look beyond your target to ensure the safety of others as well as the environment.

Whether you are free diving, using a snorkel or have scuba gear, **bubbles are the most common reason that fish swim away**. Bumping equipment together or fins hitting the sea bed or rocks create noise and vibrations that alert fish to your presence and make shooting them difficult.

# A Word About Safety

No guide to spearfishing would be complete without some basic comments regarding safety. It is important to remember that a spear gun is a potentially deadly weapon and good **spear gun etiquette** should always be observed.

- Leave the safety on until you are ready to shoot

- Never modify the safety or trigger on your gun

- Only load the gun underwater

- Never fire the spear gun in the direction of other divers, delicate structures such as coral reefs or above the water

- Pay attention to spear gun recoil to avoid a broken mask, nose or teeth.

Another important issue is general diving safety. The **use of buoys and flags** is always a good idea to alert boaters to your presence. It is never advised to spearfish alone but if you do, you should inform someone of your plans and intended location and check in at regular intervals.

When you catch one or more fish, **pay close attention to the surroundings** to see if you are attracting the attention of predators. The blood and thrashing movement of the fish alert sharks to the presence of food! It would be a shame to share your catch with a shark and a tragedy if your string of fish doesn't satisfy his appetite.

There are some simple details to keep in mind to *minimize the chance of a shark encounter* and to maximize your safety if one takes place:

- Stay in a group

- Blend in with the environment

- Avoid known feeding areas as well as spots with unusually active marine life

- Be aware of the sudden disappearance of fish

- Always face the shark and maintain eye contact

- Immediately give up your catch

- Don't corner the shark between yourself and the boat, coral or the beach

# Samba And Shallow Water Blackouts

Even the most experienced divers have run into trouble with these life threatening events so it is important to understand the danger involved with free diving. It is also a key reason for never diving alone because the presence of a buddy may be the only thing that saves your life.

The least severe form of blacking out is the loss of motor control also called **the Samba** due to the appearance of the body 'dancing'. This always occurs after the diver has reached the surface in the interval of the first breath getting oxygen to the brain. It may be as mild as a flickering of the eyes or trembling of the extremities or as violent as full-body shaking or complete loss of control. Unless the diver's ability to hold his face out of the water is compromised, recovery from this type of blackout is quick and can occur without assistance.

**A shallow water blackout** occurs within the top 35 feet (10 m) below the surface and is usually the result of the pressure change forcing the remaining oxygen out of the blood. If a diver exceeds their safe limit or has gone deeper than usual, the supply of oxygen is depleted before there is an opportunity to take a breath. This is the time when a buddy needs to pay close attention to the action of the ascending diver and jump into action if movement has stopped.

**A deep water blackout** is the most severe because it takes place below 10 m and requires emergency action by a knowledgeable rescuer.

There is no hard and fast rule about the length of time any diver can stay submerged and numerous factors play a part in altering even the most experienced diver's ability. It is crucial to be aware of your body and the many variables that affect it such as hydration, degree of stress, nutrition, rest, or altered breathing patterns. Every new location has different characteristics that can affect the conditions of the dive. The same is also true for weather factors so you must be aware of the environment. The best advice is to **stay well within the limits you have mastered and always have a buddy!**

In areas where the use of scuba gear is allowed, the diver needs to pay attention to depth and time under water so that he does not suffer from nitrogen build up in the blood. A diving watch and depth gauge help monitor this situation and there should always be a slow ascent.

One last point to remember is to **know the law regarding licenses and regulations** regarding the limits on the size or species of fish you can catch. Trouble with the Coast Guard or Fish and Game officials is the last thing you want, especially when it is so easy to avoid.

Although this is an Australian-based initiative, similar safety guidelines are published by many other spearfishing organizations and clubs.

Generally accepted **safety rules for spearfishing** include the following:

1. *Never go alone*
2. *Make a plan*
3. *Consider sea and weather conditions*
4. *Never hyperventilate*
5. *Know your limits*
6. *Never go out when tired, ill or cold*
7. *Check all your gear for wear or damage before and after you go*
8. *Perform appropriate gun cleaning and maintenance*
9. *Always be correctly weighted*
10. *Never spearfish without appropriate floats, flags and float lines*
11. *Never spearfish after consuming alcohol*
12. *Always check local conservation laws*

{ ONE UP ONE DOWN }

**One:** Dive with a buddy, and practice one up one down. This means watching your buddy dive down, and, return safely to the surface, make eye contact, a blackout can occur up to 15 seconds after ascent. If you are diving with someone not as adept as you are, stay within their comfortable limits, not yours. If you have misadventure then they are able to dive to assist you.

**Two:** Dive well within your limits – don't push yourself, no fish is worth your life.

**Three:** Dive with a rig cord and float with flag attached.

Reels have their place, but not in dirty water, rough conditions, open water or strong currents.

If you practice these simple steps, you will greatly minimize your harm while maximizing your spearfishing enjoyment.

## spear safe
AUSTRALIAN SPEARFISHING SAFETY INITIATIVE
www.spearsafe.webs.com

"Safe Spearfishing Message"

Australian Spearfishing Academy

Tuition in FreeDive Spearfishing

# CHAPTER 7 – HOT SPOTS FOR GREAT SPEARFISHING

## A Matter Of Personal Preference

Spearfishing is a popular sport all over the world, whether it is in fresh water lakes and rivers, coastal bays and inlets or the open ocean. Just as there are many reasons to enjoy spearfishing, there are many options for what people consider the best spots to participate in the sport.

Perhaps the best thing about spearfishing is that anyone can participate in the sport in virtually any body of water. All it takes is attention to the surroundings, some helpful advice from spearos familiar with the area and the interest to dive in.

For some people, spearfishing is a natural adventure best suited to rustic if not primitive conditions similar to those of ancient hunters who depended on this activity to procure food. Camping may be the most appropriate accommodations for such rugged individuals but that is certainly a matter of opinion.

Spearfishing from a boat offers a wider range of opportunities, especially if the vessel is equipped with sleeping quarters and space for equipment. Many different types of environments can be accessed easily and relatively quickly so the diver can have a variety of experiences while enjoying the advantages offered by modern amenities.

Many other people take advantage of bargain airfares and hotel packages to experience the best spearfishing locations in countless areas around the world. Spearfishing is a great vacation activity that can be enjoyed by individuals, couples and families and hotels or resorts that provide equipment and transportation are a great choice.

For still others, following different species of fish is the most enjoyable aspect of the sport and this may also include participating in tournaments and competitions all around the world. These are planned and sponsored by numerous spearfishing clubs and associations and the list of venues grows every year.

# Frequently Recommended Locations

There are factors that make some locations particularly attractive to spearos and what appeals to some will not necessarily be the ideal for others. The following list is by no means exhaustive but is intended to simply provide some ideas about specific locations and the reasons that they are popular.

**Baja, Mexico**

The Sea of Cortez (the Gulf of California) and the Pacific Ocean around Southern Baja are home to a tremendous variety of native fish species. The water is pleasantly warm and visibility is generally excellent. There are a variety of depths and underwater surface features as well as ten FADs (fish attracting devices) which are anchored offshore during the summer to provide more spearfishing zones. Common species are amberjack, blue marlin, grouper, wahoo and yellow fin tuna.

**Belize, Central America**

Located in Central America between Mexico and Guatemala on the Caribbean Sea, Belize offers access to a portion of the second largest barrier reef in the world. There are roughly 500 species of fish and over 100 types of coral that make it one of the most diverse ecosystems in the world. Many opportunities are available for novice spear fishermen but there is also plenty of excitement in the north in Shark-Ray Alley where stingrays and nurse sharks can be found.

**Caribbean Islands**

Throughout the Caribbean and nearby Atlantic, there are countless locations that abound in fish and beautiful coral formations. Hundreds of islands offer plenty of shallow areas perfect for beginners but there are also many wrecks, crevices, canyons and other underwater features that provide great spots to find trophy fish.

**Cozumel, Mexico**

Made famous by Jacques Cousteau in a 1961 documentary, the island of Cozumel allows not only advanced divers and spear fishermen plenty of opportunities to explore the 20- mile long Maya Reef but also offers shallow spots for beginners. More than 200 varieties of tropical fish including parrot fish, trumpet fish and angelfish as well as coral, sponges and seahorses make this comfortably warm, clear water home.

## Great Barrier Reef, Australia

This is probably the most well-known dive site in the world since it is the largest – it can even be seen from the Space Shuttle! This amazing environment is home to over 1500 species of fish, dolphins, sea snakes, sea turtles, rays and whales as well as 400 species of coral. Actual spearfishing is rather limited and areas are designated by colored zones for General Use, Habitat Protection and Conservation Park. Even without catching any fish, it is a spectacular experience to just enjoy the beauty and immensity of the Great Barrier Reef Marine Park.

## Indonesia

Indonesia is actually an archipelago made up of over 15,000 islands covering just over 3,000 miles (5,000 km). Fishing has been a way of life for the people of the islands for thousands of years but there are now major threats to the environment due to over-fishing, polluted run-off and urban development. In spite of this, there are still some amazing locations where spearfishing is truly magnificent such as Bali, the Lesser Sunda Islands, many of which are volcanic, and Sulawesi.

**Malaysian Borneo**

For advanced divers, Sipadan Island in the middle of the Celebes Sea in northern Borneo offers an amazing environment that is home to green and hawksbill turtles and is also known for frequent appearances of schools of mackerel and barracuda along with hammerhead and whale sharks. The island is made up of living coral sitting on top of an extinct volcano and offers a diverse sea floor full of exciting features.

**Maui, Hawaii**

Under water lava formations make snorkeling and spearfishing along the Molokini Crater quite interesting, especially with a 250 foot (75 m) vertical wall. Marine species include many different fish, eagle rays, sea turtles and small reef sharks and even whales in season. Fish that are specifically targeted around Maui include Peacock Grouper, Blacktail Snapper, Giant Trevally, Orange Spine Unicorn and Milkfish, to name just a few.

**Sharm El Sheikh**

At the Ras Mohammed National Park located on the southern tip of the Sinai Peninsula, there are abundant coral reefs in many colors and shapes that are home to clownfish, sea eels and black tip reef sharks. Wrecks and caves provide plenty of sites to explore and strong currents and deep drop offs offer excitement to advanced divers. Drift dives are among the most popular options in the area due to tidal flow and currents.

**Sub-Arctic Ice Fishing**

For the truly hardy, free diving spearfishing does take place under the ice in Alaska and in fresh water along the northern border of the US. It is extremely demanding and dangerous but for real thrill-seekers, it provides a great rush. Much more common, however, is spearfishing through the ice, just like ancient mankind performed to provide food throughout the long winter months. This type of ice fishing is traditionally done in a darkened shanty so that the fish that come along to inspect a decoy suspended through the hole can be seen and speared – hence the name *Darkhouse Spearfishing*.

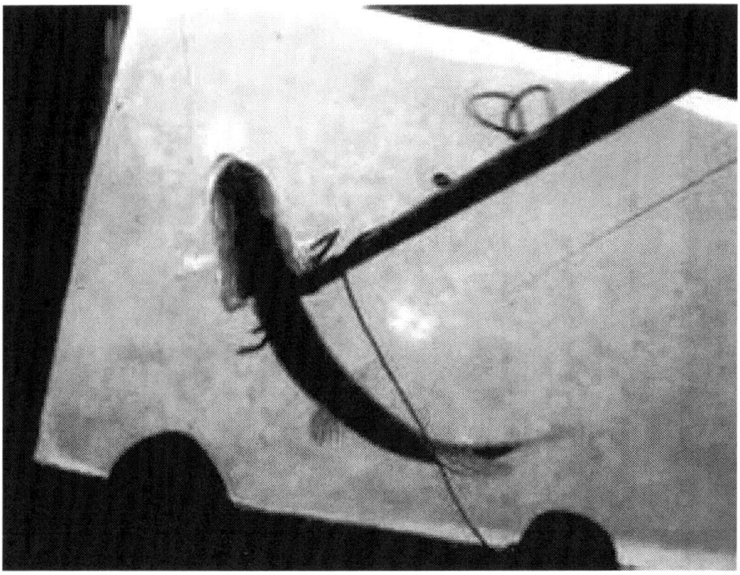

# CONCLUSION

Spearfishing is a terrific activity for many different reasons. It provides plenty of action and excitement as well as a way to connect with nature and enjoy the beauty and tranquility of the undersea environment. With so many places to go spearfishing and different types of fish to catch, it also provides a reason to travel the globe.

Whether in sea or fresh water, spearfishing has enthusiasts in virtually every country in the world. For thousands of years, men have used the same basic techniques and equipment to supply food for the family and participate in sport. Geographic location and climate conditions don't affect the outcome – tropical warmth or sub-arctic cold are both venues for some type of spearfishing.

Although the basic concept of spearfishing has not changed in millennia, there are now many new materials from which spear guns, shafts and tips are made which make them stronger, lighter and more durable. Additional equipment such as wetsuits, weights, floats and lines add comfort and safety to the sport and allow for extended time in the water in pursuit of the perfect catch.

Equipment is easy to find and good advice comes from plenty of sources. Marinas and sporting goods stores as well as shops that specialize in fishing gear have knowledgeable staff that can offer suggestions and help make comparisons. Online blogs and the websites of spearfishing organizations also provide plenty of information about all aspects of the sport.

Just as with any sport, a certain degree of physical fitness is required for successful spearfishing but there are also plenty of modifications for people with less than optimal health or swimming capability. Many organizations provide guides and lessons to help people learn the safest, most secure ways to enjoy the sport within the context of their abilities.

Whether you want to explore the depths of the ocean with blue water diving, stay closer to shore with boat or shore diving or find freshwater treasures in the depths of lakes or under the ice, there is a the perfect spear gun and gear for you within a wide range of prices.

For the truly dedicated, competitive spear fisherman, annual tournaments and other spearfishing events are held in locations in many different countries for both ocean and freshwater spearfishing. Even for amateurs, several organizations post the sizes of record catches on their websites.

Now is the perfect time to find out what this tremendous sport has to offer! With the advice in this book and some help from reputable shop keepers, you can get started with the basics and discover just how rewarding the sport of spearfishing really is. Who knows what adventures you may have as you join in the hunt for the elusive 'big one' or the most beautiful undersea location!

# ABOUT THE AUTHOR

Mike McGuire has been spearfishing for his entire life. Growing up beside the ocean, he had endless opportunities to scuba and fish, becoming acquainted at an early age with fishing and freediving. He began fishing with his father, at a very young age, enjoying the spray of the water over the side of the boat. Once he was old enough to scuba dive, his father (a scuba instructor) began taking Mike on freediving excursions, and once he was comfortable in the water, they brought along the spearguns. Not only did he enjoy spending time with his father, he genuinely enjoyed swimming in the ocean and the sport of hunting down the perfect fish for dinner.

Ever since he was a boy, Mike has spent the majority of his life in the water, traveling all over the world to fish in the best waters, and talking to other spearfishermen about their equipment and technique. As he has accumulated this information, he began testing it out, documenting it, making a note of what was sound advice, and what didn't hold water. Through years of trial and error, he began to uncover the best places to fish, the best depths, and the best freediving and spearfishing equipment, even winning a few competitions along the way.

As he spoke with those experienced in spearfishing, he saw a need for a book that could not only quickly teach men the sport of spearfishing, but also provide a safety, gear, and technique refresher to those who had been diving and fishing for years.

All of the advice in his book has been thoroughly field tested by Mike McGuire himself. This compilation of knowledge is a result of years of experience and working with other spearfishing and freediving experts. Throughout this process, Mike became especially fascinated with the easiest way to teach others to spearfish. As he talked with people that had never done the sport, he realized that most of them were daunted by the concept, and that it seemed too complicated to learn.

Over the years, however, he had come to understand that spearfishing and freediving were actually easy sports, something that could be easily learned and passed on, if those who wished to learn it were provided with only the best information and advice. His philosophy has always been to keep it simple and to keep it clean. His long process of trial and error has taught Mike that it is alright to fail, as long as you keep trying and don't complicate a simple sport with too much flash and flair.

All of his knowledge, spearfishing philosophy, and years of expertise have been brought together in one easy to follow, fun to read book.

Printed in Great Britain
by Amazon